How to Be a Good Role Model for Your Child

Johanna Fisher, Ph.D.,
and Penelope B. Grenoble, Ph.D.

CB

CONTEMPORARY
BOOKS

CHICAGO · NEW YORK

ACKNOWLEDGMENTS

Special thanks to Keshav Kamath, who worked on the preparation of this manuscript, and Creighton Grenoble for computer assistance.

—PBG

CONTENTS

ParentBooks That Work Series   v

Introduction   ix

Part I
Influences
on Role Modeling   1

Part II
Your Role as a
Parent and How It
Affects Your Child   13

Part III
Some Strategies for
Maximizing Your
Role Modeling   39

Conclusion   77

References   79

An Introduction to *ParentBooks That Work*

It has been said that twenty-five-dollar words can be used to cover up twenty-five-cent ideas. In our increasingly technological society, jargon and complex language often confuse the meaning of information. This is particularly the case in the social and psychological sciences.

The "hard sciences" such as physics, chemistry, and biology have an advantage: there is little chance, for example, that a photon or a quark will be confused with something else.

In the human sciences, however, we have at least two problems with language. One is that the popular definition of a word such as *sex* or *intelligence* can differ considerably from the way a professional in the field might use it. Although we parents share a common pool of language with social scientists and teachers and therapists, words like *input* and *reinforcement, expectations* and *assessment,* mean one thing to parents and another to social science experts. Thus the danger that we will not understand each other is very real.

The human sciences' other language problem is jargon. A particular group of human scientists may develop obscure or seemingly incomprehensible language as a shortcut to communication among its members. Thus, jargon can be a roadblock when the experts try to talk to people outside their field.

The books in this series are the result of skillful collaboration between trained psychologists experienced in family and child development and a seasoned writer. The authors have strived to take twenty-five-dollar ideas and deliver them in language that is clear, concise, and most useful to you. In these six books, the emphasis is on presenting intelligent and practical ideas that you can use to help solve the age-old problems of child rearing.

This brings us to the very reason for these books. It might have occurred to you to ask, "Why should I rely on so-called experts when I can fall back on tradition and conventional wisdom? After all, the human race has survived well on what parents have taught children through the ages." Think about that for a moment. In the long history of human life on this planet, most of our energy has been spent in survival against the elements. It's only in most recent history that we've enjoyed the luxury to live, rather than simply survive. The fact is that the help and advice children need most nowadays has to do with a different level of survival in a world we've created ourselves, a complex world of rapid change.

Even though at moments nature can remind us of her often terrible wrath and power, most of our problems are still manmade. What we—parents and children both—have to learn is to deal with a reality that we have created ourselves.

In the bewildering array of cultures, creeds, and cross-purposes that are modern life, we need a special set of skills to live and be productive. Competition is an essential fact of life. Your child faces stress and pressure from society's expectations from the day he or she is born. To get through, your child needs the best help you can give.

The position of the professional expert is new and revered in our society. The expert is one of our cleverest inventions. Involved in the intense study of one problem or subject, the expert comes to know it better than anyone else. We trust the expert because we know that we don't have the time or ability to sort out everything ourselves. And, if the expert follows the best instincts of his profession, his high level of professional competence will serve you. By using the specialized knowledge of the expert, parents can face the difficult but practical problems of building a family and preparing their children to meet the demands of early childhood and elementary school.

Enlightened by this advice, we can give our children a healthy attitude and a better chance.

These concise and practical books deal with some of the most important issues in young children's lives today. They will help you to help your child and to feel good about your role as a parent. With this in mind, we dedicate this series to you.

Richard H. Thiel, Ph.D.
California State University

INTRODUCTION

*H*ow to be a good role model for your child. A simple phrase, but what exactly does it mean? Most parents, if they think about it for a minute, think about role modeling as something to consider only as their children grow up. They usually think of sex roles, which is why we give dolls to female children and hammers and saws to males. Or of future jobs and vocations—which means a nurse's uniform for the girl, a doctor's kit to the boy.

The truth is that if you wait until you can teach your child—girl or boy—how to pour hot water from a play teapot or pound a wooden nail with a plastic hammer, you have dallied too long in providing a good model. Most parents don't realize how important their own actions (and their interaction as a couple) are in developing their children's character and personality. The fact is that we act as models for our children every day of our lives from the day our children are born. Children are acutely attuned to our behavior and will take cues from it as they attempt to determine their own actions.

This does not mean that you should ignore your own needs while catering to your child's demands. Far from it. You can never be a good parent if you are frustrated, and you should never lose sight of having your own life to lead. However, you need to be aware of how your behavior influences the behavior of your child. Being a good role model for your child should not be a thankless process. Rather, it should be an outgrowth of your own growth and development as an individual and as one member of the family team.

The most powerful force shaping your child's personality is his identification with you as his parent. Traditionally, home and family made up the total world for most children during the preschool years. In today's society, however, many children are enrolled in day-care centers long before they go to school. There they meet authority figures—parent substitutes—outside of their immediate family. Other children have substitute caretakers in the home. If either is the case in your family, don't despair. Even if your child spends a lot of time outside of your direct supervision, even at an early age, it is not a cause for anxiety if the time you do spend with him is quality time.

By quality we mean that you are *actively* involved with your child in ways that make him feel good about himself and enhance his feelings of self-worth and self-esteem. Quality time is not for scolding, threatening, or punishing. Nor is it for preparing dinner, entertaining adult friends, and virtually ignoring your child. Quality time is devoted to positive interactions between you and your child. It is a time for such mutually pleasurable activities as story-telling, reading, games, or just listening patiently and attentively as your child expresses how he feels. Most important, quality time involves physical closeness between you and your child—hugging, kissing, or just sitting side by side.

From the earliest years, your child will watch you to see how you act. He observes how you deal with other members of the family—with each other, with his brothers and sisters, aunts and uncles—and with people from the outside world. Your child will imitate you and what you do, starting in early childhood through adolescence. In homes where parents are considerate of each other's feelings, a child will value and develop that attitude; when parents are tense and anxious, he is likely to be fearful and scared.

Parents who have taken time with their children and have been able to teach them a sense of their values can feel confident that their children will continue to stick to those values even as they leave the home—be that at two or twenty. Even as your child first enters school, your behavior will affect him more strongly than other outside influences. You will continue to be your child's primary role model for as long as you are part of his life. You are the person whose behavior, interests, and attitudes your child will attempt to imitate from the day he is born.

Thus, waiting until you can talk about these things with your child is too late. Children are very quick. It therefore behooves you—perhaps even before you have children—to take a look at your lifestyle and your values. Assess your interests and beliefs and pinpoint what you wish to model for your child. The information presented in this book will help you do that.

As in all books in this series, we typically refer to a child using male pronouns, such as he and his. Please keep in mind that we are also thinking of your daughter, who today faces considerable challenges in structuring her role in society.

Part I
Influences
on Role Modeling

If you were to stop the average person on the street today and ask him to name one of the worst parts of life in contemporary society, the answer would probably be *stress*. We live in an era characterized by tension and anxiety—too much to do in too little time and too many demands, complicated by feelings of personal inadequacy. Our society is one of intense competition, rapid change, and an uncertain future. These conditions encourage a high level of stress and influence the social relationships that are essential to our existence. The challenges of a society in which change is everywhere, where lives are easily disrupted, and where social values and goals seem to be in a continual state of flux are difficult enough for adults. Children growing up in such a society face an even more difficult task. They need all the help they can get to grow and develop. Their difficulties are complicated by a number of social developments.

1. LOSS OF THE EXTENDED FAMILY

A child growing up today lacks the soft cushion of the extended family—close relationships with brothers, sisters, aunts, uncles, and grandparents. Traditionally, members of the extended family took some of the burden from busy parents and helped immensely in the task of role modeling. Due to such factors as increased family mobility and a higher divorce rate, this is no longer true.

Unfortunately, at the same time the family's influence over children has diminished, expectations for their behavior are becoming more complicated and, simultaneously, more vague. In effect, what is happening in our overloaded society is that the time available for you to devote to child rearing is more limited and more rushed than ever before, while social pressures are urging your child to grow up too fast. You must face this unfortunate fact. In our stressful and intensely competitive society, many things compete for your attention—and often at your child's expense.

Against this background, it falls to the much-reduced nuclear family—mother and father, and more often single parents—to provide the guidelines for a child's character and personality. Even in families where both parents live in the home, there may be the additional complication of two careers. This means that because both parents are outside of the home during the day and sometimes into the evening, children are watched by substitute caretakers or, even more disturbing, may be left unsupervised for long periods of time. A very fundamental and negative result from this decreased parent-child contact is not enough time for you to model the behavior you expect of your child and for your child to absorb whatever modeling you do provide.

Your child is looking for security in this fluid society; he is searching for clues to guide him. To aid him you must make the commitment to yourself and your child that the time you spend together will be that special kind of quality time. Selected, superior time spent between parent and child can indeed make up for diminished quantity of time. This applies to all aspects of child rearing, but especially to the all-important activity of role modeling. If you pay little attention to your child during the time you spend with him or if you are inconsistent in your own behavior and the behavior you encourage or reprimand him for, there is no doubt that your child will suffer.

In an inconsistent world, your home should supply your child with a sense of security and stability—which he needs to develop high self-esteem—stability that is based on the values you present. If you aren't consistent, your child receives mixed messages. Children often feel that parents who are vague about behavioral expectations do not really care about them. Worse yet are parents who set rules and then break those rules themselves. If watching TV is not allowed during meals, then it must be so for everyone—from children watching Saturday morning cartoons during breakfast to parents watching the evening news at dinner. A parent who violates rules but will not allow his child to do so is only asking for trouble. Your child will harbor resentment against such double standards and may come to think all rules are irrational. If you lay down ground rules and then do not enforce those rules, or change them on whim, you can expect your child to keep pushing to find out where the real limits are.

2. PROBLEMS OF WORKING PARENTS

If you're employed outside the home, you probably come home both tired and stressed from the demands made on you during the day. You may still be preoccupied by what happened at the office and may require time to wind down. But wind down you must, because once you are at home, you need to switch gears and think about the needs of your child. One of the greatest errors parents commit is bringing their work home with them (something spouses have complained about for centuries) and allowing job problems to occupy their emotional energy during their time at home with the family. Children often have already spent long hours in a day-care center and need attention from you. Even a well-designed and well-staffed day-care center cannot make up for the bonding that is needed, especially at an early age, between yourself and your child.

3. FAMILY MOBILITY

It is a fact of modern life that families are more mobile than ever before. With every move, children are uprooted from friendships and familiar neighborhoods and are faced with the challenge of breaking into already established groups in a new environment. This becomes a problem for children age four and over, who are seeking their first relationships with peers, and it becomes more of a challenge as the child gets older. Since younger children engage only in what is known as "parallel play," in which they associate with other children but don't interact in a way that establishes solid friendships, a child of five might not have much difficulty moving to a new neighborhood. But by age seven children will likely have formed a network of friends, at least in the immediate neighborhood, so that it will not only be difficult to break away from these associations but perhaps even more of a struggle to establish new friendships in a different locale.

Your child must have a very firm sense of self-worth and a solid value system if he is to be accepted by a new group of peers. If a child in a highly mobile family is shy and retiring, he may find moving to a new neighborhood traumatic. Unable to make contact with other children, and without the proper help from his parents, the child may become isolated and develop into a loner, withdrawing still further. On the other hand, a child's need for friends may be so great that he is willing to set aside his family's values to buy into new peer groups. How much your child gives up depends on how strong the bonding with you has been and on how much of that bond must be exchanged for friendship.

By *bonding* we are referring to the all-important ties between your child and yourself or other parent figures in his environment. A child who has ample evidence of his parents' love for him—whose feeling of self-worth directly reflects his parents' belief in his worthiness—will identify with those parents. He will want to associate with his parents and adopt his parents' values, goals, and even personality styles. The stronger the bonding between you and your child, the more effective your role modeling is in supporting your child's sense of self-esteem. This will in turn enhance his capacity to develop new friendships while keeping close to his family's values and personal values within his peer contacts.

4. ALTERNATIVE ROLE MODELS

One unfortunate result of diminished time that parents and children spend with each other is that a child left to his own devices may take to imitating the behavior of adults outside the home. Although this always happens to some degree as a child forms attachments to favorite teachers, scout leaders, or even a media star, if it happens at too early an age, it can be bad. The child is likely to become confused for two reasons: first, the nonfamily role model may suggest values that are different from the child's family's; second, it is unlikely that such a person would be able to provide the child the input and guidance that he needs. A little experimentation with adult models outside the home is not to be discouraged, however, as long as it is undertaken with a strong foundation in the values and attitudes of the family.

5. INFLUENCE OF TELEVISION

Much has been said about both the positive and negative influences of television. Research indicates that it can cause both beneficial and destructive effects in our society. For young children, large amounts of television viewing are not good for later stages of development, both physiologically and psychologically.

Nathan Fox, in a study published in *Optometric Weekly*, suggests that because television images move while the viewer's eyes remain relatively stationary, if your child watches several hours of TV a day, his eye muscles will fail to develop the strength required for reading and other vision-oriented tasks. Research has shown that first-graders who spent extensive amounts of time in early years watching television were unable to scan a printed page because their eye muscles were underdeveloped.

Television is neither a consistent nor good source for modeling adults' or children's behavior. The range of shows currently on most channels presents a confusing spectrum of values and actions, and the images used in advertising add to the problem. Many shows fail to present logical consequences of characters' actions, which children may easily (and dangerously) misinterpret. An example of this is cartoons, in which one character annihilates another or is blown up but returns unscathed in the next sequence.

Although this is the age of telecommunications and TV is a fact, if not a necessity, of life, TV watching can further eat away at the precious time that families should spend together. Working parents may use the television as an in-house baby-sitter; others may see TV as an occasional stand-in that allows them to attend to such tasks as cooking or cleaning. It is, however, far too easy to fall into the habit of associating with the television instead of other family members.

The fact that there are now more families in which both parents work is a very serious threat to generations born and reared with less contact with their parents. We have not begun to see the results of this. This does not mean they are irreversible, however. We offer here some suggestions to help you— whether you are a working parent, single parent, or a member of a dual-career couple—take advantage of your own time, talent, and skills to model the best behavior for your child within the time you do spend with him. By being a good role model for your child, you will help him be the best he can be.

Given the various facts of contemporary life, your role in patterning values, attitudes, and correct behavioral models for your child has become more important than ever—even as conflicting demands for your time have increased. In the two sections that follow, we offer some hints on what to look for in your family that will help you assess your capacity to be a good role model for your child. As with all problems you encounter raising a family, there are consequences for children who for some reason or another have not been prepared with good role modeling in their family. The goal of this book is to aid you in preventing these problems before they happen, to help you understand just what role modeling is, and to help you feel comfortable with your responsibilities. We hope that after reading it you will be better prepared to get your child off to a good start in this stressful, ambiguous, often confusing society that we all must live in.

Part II
Your Role as a Parent and How It Affects Your Child

It is useful to take a closer look at what we mean when we say *role modeling*. We all play a number of roles throughout our lifetime. Some are because of our chronological age, some are related to our social position, others to achievement; some we assume by choice, some by design, and some are forced upon us. Society prescribes how we are to act in any given social situation, which in turn is affected by the requirements of the role we play in that situation.

Thus you may assume the role of a parent at the same time you are the director of a nuclear physics lab or the chairman of a local chamber music society—or you may be all three. You may be the leader of the group or its black sheep. You may be your family's prodigal son, your grandfather's special granddaughter, and your brother's favorite sibling at the same time you must fulfill the role of your company's most successful stockbroker. Each role will make a demand on you to act appropriately. Or you may choose to act inappropriately. To the extent that your family provided you with good models and values, you will be able to meet the needs your various roles require of you, and you will be able to move from role to role with a certain ease and aplomb. (At least, that's the theory.)

When we speak of role modeling for your child, however, we are talking of something much more basic. We are referring to modeling on a much more primitive level of intuition, imitation, and assimilation of values, attitudes, and behavior. This happens at so subtle a level that you may not even be aware of it. The younger your child, the more this applies. Forget the tea sets and hammers and start thinking of the kind of person you would like your child to be as an adult and by what means you can help achieve that. And start doing this even before your child is born.

This doesn't mean, of course, that if you already have growing children there is nothing you can do to influence them by offering a positive image of a productive, caring, feeling adult. It is only that the job is easier—as are all child-rearing activities—the earlier you start and the more you know about who you are and what *you* want out of life for yourself and your child.

Perhaps more than any of the other challenges faced by you in the child-rearing process, role modeling reflects directly on *your* behavior, primarily in the home. This parent-child relationship is a complex interaction, and it requires an understanding of its dynamics, along with a few words of caution. Unlike many other difficulties your child may experience in his developing years, the problem of inadequate or inappropriate role modeling may not be obvious from your child's behavior. You may be more effective by evaluating yourself and *your* behavior. Sometimes we become so involved with the problems and difficulties of our lives—its challenges and rewards—that we neglect the trees for the forest. So please read this section with care. If your child has role difficulties, it may be a reflection of your personal problems that are affecting the atmosphere in your home. Think how nice it will be to solve two problems at the same time.

THE CHALLENGES OF PARENTING

Being a parent, and thus being a role model, is a double-edged sword. Your child will copy bad or destructive behavior as quickly as he will imitate constructive, positive behavior. This places lots of responsibility on you. You must ask yourself, "What kind of adult do I want my child to become?" You must then shape yourself and model the behavior, values, and attitudes you want from your child.

It is virtually impossible for you to attempt to convince your child to "do what I say, not what I do." Children will do what they see adults doing. You may repeatedly instruct your child never to tell a lie; but if he observes you and your spouse constantly telling lies or deceiving one another, he will model your actions. Your *behavior* is the significant message.

By age five a child's personality is already well defined. This means that your child's character is well developed even before he enters the school setting. And where has it come from? From you and from the home you've established. By *personality* we mean your child's approach to the world, demonstrated most often by outward behavior—whether, for example, he is confident and outgoing or timid, shy, and withdrawn. An angry, aggressive child sees the world as hostile, which reinforces his aggressive personality. A calm, self-confident child uses his energies to create and explore, and the satisfaction resulting from these activities motivates him still further. By age five you can identify these characteristics in your child. In a kindergarten class an angry child who is hostile to his friend is showing behavior that, unless corrected, may lead to problems as a teenager. On the other hand, a child who has been raised in a strict, disciplined atmosphere may seem outwardly submissive but is resentful inside. He may look harmless, but he will be underhandedly aggressive, even at age five. A happy child who was allowed to explore and create in safety will not exhibit these negative behaviors.

Since by age five such characteristics are already established, they will dictate how your child interacts with his world, especially in school. Thus, your child's experience in the early school years stems from the traits he brings with him from home. What your child understands as your family's attitudes and values from infancy to age five will greatly affect his success in school, as well as his social relationships.

Your child's self-concept, especially in these early

years, is formed based on how you treat him. The more a child's worth is validated, the stronger he will identify with your value system and the more influence you will have on his behavior—and the more certain you can be of what he will do and what he will become in later life.

You should know, however, that although your child may try to be independent by seeming to disregard some of your values, this is merely a normal pattern of growth and development. If you have provided a loving and nurturing environment and have acted as a consistent and positive role model, your child will stick with what he learned from you.

For example, an adolescent may choose to rebel by wearing strange clothes or by forming close bonds with friends you may not necessarily like or understand. Unless the teenager's behavior violates well-entrenched family values, this should not be considered a significant problem. If, for instance, ownership of possessions has been respected in the family, you can be relatively assured that your child will not steal. Likewise, if aggression is not part of your family's behavior, your child is unlikely to be violent or aggressive. *In other words, the fundamental values you have modeled will remain intact as your child grows, and he will choose to rebel only in trivial matters. Obviously, time spent on modeling desirable behavior is an investment well worth making.*

And so good role modeling is preventive. By the time you become aware that your child is acting inappropriately, by failing in school, being truant, stealing, or lying, it may be too late to address the problems through positive role modeling alone; professional help might be needed. Family therapy is the most appropriate form of help. If therapy becomes necessary, you should see it as an opportunity, rather than a negative experience. It will provide everyone in the family a chance to sort out the difficulties that caused the problems. It is not a matter of "fixing the kid" or "curing the child." Your child's difficulty is part of how your family members act with each other. Thus, as in any other family matter, the whole family must work together toward resolution.

As you evaluate your family life, whether you now have children or are contemplating a family, you might find it useful to follow the six following suggestions to determine how prepared you are to be the right kind of role model for your child.

1. BEGIN EARLY

As we said in the introduction, many parents feel they don't have to be conscious of their behavior until their children are older. Researchers and therapists, however, are discovering that children pick up behavior much earlier than originally thought. Evidence now suggests that parents should start watching their own behavior immediately at their child's birth—not three years down the road when the child begins to develop bad behavior or to demonstrate undesirable personality traits.

You might even do well to "practice" before you have a child. It has recently been suggested, for example, that even in the womb the fetus can hear its mother's voice and may experience the sound as a source of comfort. A mother who is happy about her pregnancy and takes the time to sing or speak in a soft, comforting tone to her unborn child has a far more positive effect than a mother who is constantly anxious and yells at those around her. Infants only a few days old recognize and respond to their mother's voice, which implies that they have in fact been hearing that voice for some time. A valuable opportunity to influence the emotions of a newborn infant may be at the mother's disposal even before birth.

An expecting mother also needs to understand that the hormones circulating throughout her body are shared by her unborn child. The chemical effects of being excessively anxious throughout her pregnancy may be transferred to her unborn baby. (We are speaking here not of the normal anxiety that often accompanies pregnancy but of such stress as not wanting the pregnancy or a troubled relationship with your spouse.) Thus, even before birth, you help form your child's personality. Differences in newborn babies in the maternity ward may indicate they were born with some behaviors developed in the womb. Even at this age, they are already manifesting primitive personality traits. Some lie comfortably in their cribs after they have just undergone the trauma of birth, while others are restless and screaming and seem unable to achieve any solace. *An infant who seems constantly uncomfortable and irritable or is difficult to calm and sooth with physical expressions of love and caring is a child who may be in danger of suffering from tensions and anxieties later in life.*

2. PLAN FOR LIFE AFTER BIRTH

There has been a trend in modern society for dual-career parents to feel confident in leaving their children with substitute caretakers. Because of the decline in the extended family, these people often are not family members, although they may have some degree of professional training in child rearing. The rationale is that, although both parents must be out of the home, the need for consistency in the child's environment is being met—even though it might not be one of the parents who is providing it.

Given the importance of the first part of an infant's life, however, a career woman will do well to invest in the role of primary caretaker for the first eighteen or so months after her child's birth. This short period of time will provide the child with an anchor to secure the later stages of healthy development. During these early months, an infant forms an emotional attachment with one primary caretaker, and it is important that the child's care be consistent and close in this earliest stage. And so the ideal situation for a working mother is to be with her child full-time for the first eighteen months to two years of the child's life. By that time the rudiments of personality have been developed and the child is capable of dealing with outside influences, especially if your role modeling to that point has been positive. He will have taken in enough of your value system to have the self-confidence to interact with the outside world with confidence.

Although for some families there may exist no alternative but the use of a substitute caretaker, you should be aware that during the first eighteen months of life your child requires a give-and-take attachment to a primary caretaker. For this reason it is important that your child remain in the care of one caretaker—be it a nanny or a mother-in-law—rather than several and be provided with consistent and solicitous care. (Additional discussion on this subject can be found in a companion volume, *Creating a Good Self-Image in Your Child.*)

An infant who fails to respond to outside stimulation or to make an attempt to communicate with his primary caretaker through mimicking the caretaker's behavior (smiling, giggling, etc.) may be suffering from an inconsistency in care.

If you can afford it and child-care at this age is necessary, it's preferable to hire one person to work in the home. A member of the extended family or a nanny taking care of your child in your home will provide the attachment the child needs, even though the attachment is not with his parent. By the time your child is two or two-and-a-half, day-care or nursery school has certain advantages. By that time your child is beginning to socialize and may achieve a sense of gratification through association with other children.

Under extreme circumstances, if both parents must work a certain portion of the day, traditional day-care, with one person in charge of a number of infants, may be substituted, only if it is for a short period, a few hours a day, one or two days per week. Under such circumstances a parent could make up for absence during that short period by having quality time when she is with her infant. If, however, your child is placed full-time in a day-care center before he is six months old, the child is certainly at a disadvantage. Although research has not yet determined the long-term effect of such child-care, logic indicates it is not a wise choice for healthy development. If this is likely to be the case, you should consider delaying having a family until better arrangements can be made for care of your infant.

This is not to say that modern child-care and nursery schools are necessarily negative. The important point for you to be aware of is that placing your child in that sort of environment before he is twelve to eighteen months old, and certainly before six months, has certain risks. A child at that age needs one-to-one interaction. One person attempting to take care of a number of infants is unable to provide the type of intense emotional reaction and attention that your infant needs.

As another alternative, a working parent might arrange to work a four- or five-hour day instead of eight or nine hours. Although the child will be subjected to substitute caretaking during the time the parent is at work, at least the infant will not entirely lose contact with his mother (or father if he is the primary parent). This may also be an excellent strategy for making the transition from part-time to full-time day-care.

Chronological age is not an absolute standard. Most children are well prepared for day-care or preschool by age three, others by four or four-and-a-half. There is no need, for example, to keep your child isolated in the home until the age of five out of fear of exposing him to outside influences. Preschool can be an excellent prelude to a successful kindergarten and early elementary school experience. You should use your own intuition in deciding when your child is ready for day-care. If you are unsure, consult your pediatrician, a family therapist, or other parents who have children of a similar age or experience.

One other solution for two-career households is for the father to share in the responsibilities of child rearing. Between two parents there are any number of arrangements that can fulfill a child's needs. With a little planning, responsibilities in and outside the home need not overwhelm either or both parents. Evaluate your work schedules while you are prospective parents. Perhaps you will have to make compromises in potential income in order to spend as much time as possible with your family while your child is young.

3. CHECK THE ATMOSPHERE IN YOUR HOME

One of the first things an infant absorbs is his parents' emotional responses to situations, to other people in his environment, and to himself. In homes where parents are considerate of each other's needs and feelings, even very young children will respond and develop the same way. In a home where parents are tense and anxious, children may react by developing their own anxieties—even in the earliest stages of childhood. At least one researcher (Harry Sullivan in *The Interpersonal Theory of Psychiatry*) has maintained that an infant nursing at his mother's breast can pick up signs of anxiety and will become anxious himself. We all know that having a friend who is upset or anxious about something can cause us to experience a similar emotion. An infant is even more acutely attuned to the emotional nuances of the world around him. Generally, a normal child who is exposed to an anxious primary caretaker will become anxious at a very early age. Conversely, if the primary caretaker is calm, the child will experience a sense of tranquility and well-being. In homes where parents are loving, supportive, friendly and forgiving, the children respond and are likely to be loving and friendly also.

An infant exposed to anxious parents will display his discomfort by being a fussy eater, being unable to sleep, or crying a great deal for no apparent reason. An anxious child, for example, may experience persistent nightmares that cause him to wake up crying. Such an infant may also exhibit signs of fear of separation from his mother. He may cry when his mother is not physically present or when he is cared for by someone other than his mother, or he may make constant demands for the attention of his mother. This should be considered normal only until approximately twenty-four months of age. (For a further discussion of age-appropriate behavior, see the companion volume *Creating a Good Self-Image in Your Child.*)

Anxiety is not the only cause of anguish and distress in an infant. A parent who is unhappy for some reason—for example, a mother who is dissatisfied with giving up her career to care for her child—will be unable to reach out and establish good bonding with her child. A mother who feels unfulfilled as a homemaker and wishes to do something else will not be able to reach out lovingly to her husband or to the child. In such cases, it may be wise for the parent, or the couple, to reassess their situation or to seek therapy.

Parents' constant bickering and fighting may affect a child without parents' realizing it because the child may demonstrate the effects of his parents' behavior only outside the home. Susan and Eileen's parents, for example, were continually hostile toward one another. Occasionally their feelings would break out into a serious confrontation but mostly took the form of low-level antagonism on trivial issues. The two girls soon learned that their best strategy was to stay out of the way during these arguments, especially if a real blowup occurred. Avoidance, however, was not the girls' only form of coping strategy. Susan, the older girl, became very shy and quiet outside the home—an extension of her behavior in the family, where she was obedient and compliant. Eileen, four years younger, decided on a course of mild rebellion. She basically stuck to the rules of the home, but when she was outside of her parents' control she developed a reputation for creating problems—never really getting into trouble, but acting inappropriately enough to bring attention to herself. Neither child, of course, was acting defiantly. They were simply attempting to cope with their parents' behavior. Even Eileen's occasional pranks were never considered a behavior problem by teachers or other adult supervisors. Both girls, however, subsequently had a very difficult time in male-female relationships.

Feelings of tension and anxiety in your home may distress your child and cause lifelong patterns of bad role behavior. Any unresolved tension or stress in the family will influence your child and become part of his self-concept and personality. The way you interact with your spouse, as well as how you interact with your child, establishes a pattern for your child. A child who constantly is exposed to anxiety will not develop the self-confidence necessary to succeed in the world of school.

Susan and Eileen's experience illustrates another point about negative role modeling in families. If the first child is aggressive and is reprimanded, the next child is likely to be timid. If the first is timid, the second will be more aggressive, since he sees that the first isn't getting anywhere with timidity. This behavior exists below the level of awareness; your child will make an intuitive decision from what he sees happening in the family.

If your child is very shy, retiring, and tearful in school and is afraid to ask when he doesn't understand what's going on or if he's intimidated by other children, his experience in school is likely to be negative. He may begin to fail. The self-confident child, on the other hand, succeeds in the school setting, which encourages his outgoing, confident nature.

4. EVALUATE YOUR OWN BEHAVIOR
Once you have assessed the values and motivations behind your patterns of behavior, it is important to

monitor how you actually behave, not only at home but also in social situations in which you and your child are involved. Children reared by supportive, accepting parents tend to develop into self-aware adults capable of long-term goals. They are able to engage in constructive self-criticism, and they cherish their relationships with their family. In contrast, children whose parents are overly critical, authoritarian, and harsh often turn into self-absorbed adults, whose impulsiveness can lead to violence and substance abuse.

You must realize that child rearing will make demands to alter your life, in terms of not only scaling down your leisure activities but also the type of behavior you would like to see your child imitate. This is particularly true regarding discipline. Parents with quick tempers, who easily break into abusive language and physical threats or punishment when frustrated, model an aggressive mode of behavior that a child quickly assimilates. A child reared under those conditions will verbally abuse and physically attack other children. The more the child is physically punished for such behavior, the more that aggressiveness will become entrenched in his personality.

You may be conveying double messages at a more subtle level. Scolding your child for doing something he has seen you do on a number of occasions will only confuse him and will have no effect on his behavior. The same is true when you insist that your child be polite and well behaved but covertly take delight in his mischief, saying, "Oh, but wasn't it cute?" or "That's my boy." In one case you are saying one thing, while doing the opposite. In the other you are verbalizing two different things: telling your child to behave one way but in the next breath positively reinforcing him for just having behaved the opposite way.

Parents who are so involved with their own lives and problems that they have little time and energy to invest in their child may convey a variety of other double messages. An example might be a parent who says, "I love you," but because of work or other personal reasons, ignores or rejects the child. Or in a home where parents resent each other, one encourages the child to rebel against the other's authority, while insisting that the child obey his own orders. A child in a home with double messages has no sense of security. Confusion reigns, and he is at risk for serious emotional disturbances. It is therefore important to monitor both your own behavior and what you tell your child that you expect from him. Behave as you would have him behave and say what you mean.

A child who violates basic family values (say, by physically attacking other children even though in the home physical violence is abhorred), something is seriously wrong—and not necessarily with your child. More than likely, some unresolved issue exists between you and your spouse, and you should seek counseling for yourselves. What was happening to Eileen and Susan, for example, was that the two girls were simply responding to the unacknowledged hostility that existed between their parents. In such cases a professional therapist can help identify the source of your child's disturbance. Positive role modeling alone at this point would most likely be inadequate.

5. KNOW YOUR LIMITS AND SEEK PROFESSIONAL HELP WHEN NECESSARY

As your child grows into adolescence, you may be dismayed to find that the good rapport and sense of family integrity that existed up to this point seem to disintegrate. A child at this age is beset by hormonal changes and changes in physical size, intellectual development, and experience. This forces him into a new relationship with you. Long before adolescence, however, you should understand that it is not necessarily parental authority that draws your child to his family; it is the emotional bonding that has occurred through a sense of shared experiences, attitudes, and values. A child who has experienced his parents as caring for him will care about his parents. This bonding will have more effect than threats and punishments.

If you and your child have formed strong bonds of caring, he will have developed a secure enough sense of self to handle adolescence. If you have spent time being positive and encouragingly respecting your child, he will face the teen years with a fairly solid sense of self, which can help make the teenage years an interesting time. If your home is such a gratifying place that friendships do not assume an overriding importance, your child will seek associations that do not require him to act against family values. He will not sacrifice them for the sake of friends.

It is when bonding between parent and child has not been strong that peers become too important. It is then that a child will do anything—steal, use drugs, engage in destructive behavior—to gain approval of his friends. *If your child seems to be extremely susceptible to peer pressure and the behavior of the peer group is conspicuously counter to family-sanctioned behavior, your child may be experiencing role modeling problems.* A child with a poor sense of self and with weak family bonds will value peers so much that he will feel he has to do whatever they do. (For a more complete discussion of this subject, see the companion volume *Teaching Your Child to Handle Peer Pressure.*) *If by mid-adolescence you and your child are experiencing constant conflict in your home, you have not provided adequate behavioral modeling.*

Unfortunately, problems that surface in adolescence are difficult, if not impossible, to reverse. This is when you need to know your limits. A child at any age who persistently rebels against basic principles of his parents' behavior—who commits such consistently antisocial acts as lying, stealing, constantly defying authority—needs professional help. A child who is suddenly failing in school, is truant from school, or runs away from home is crying out for help. A child who sets fires or experiments with drugs or alcohol needs professional intervention. When a child has been mistreated or ignored, he will purposely reject everything his parents believe in, as made apparent to him through their lifestyle and home behavior. If he has been mistreated at home, he will act up in school. Such a child is in trouble; the family is in trouble. If he has been consistently rebelling, it's too late to practice good role modeling to counteract the problem.

Children who have not been encouraged during childhood will struggle with problems of self-worth throughout adolescence. Additionally, as adults they will seek to prove to themselves that they really have value. Sadly, they may never be able to do so. Such individuals may become workaholics, who, no matter how successful they are, must continue to prove themselves, while at the same time they continue to hear their parents saying, "You're no good." Although as an adult it is possible to use success in the adult world to gain a sense of self-worth, the scars of childhood may always be there. Parents must remember that an adolescent has not yet achieved a sufficient degree of adult success to generate that sense of self-worth, and they must start early in a child's life to ensure that he grows and matures with a positive sense of his own self-worth.

6. BE AWARE OF YOUR ROLE IN GENDER IDENTIFICATION

Although we continue to move toward equality of the sexes, there are still clear-cut expectations for behavior associated with gender. The more closely your son identifies with his father, or your daughter with her mother, the more comfortable each will be with himself or herself as a member of that sex in society. Your child will know how to interact with his peers if he has learned to identify with the parent of the same sex. This is especially true when your child enters puberty. He learns not only how to interact with people of the same sex but also how he as a member of one sex is expected to interact with members of the opposite sex.

Your daughter will learn feminine mannerisms from her mother, while your son, if he identifies easily with his father, will be able to enjoy his masculine role in the world and will feel confident in friendships with other boys. A boy who has not established a strong emotional bond with an adult male is ambivalent about how to interact with other boys, and they will immediately sense it. They may tease and torment such a boy. A father who is preoccupied with his career at the expense of spending time with his son places him at risk. In homes where single mothers are raising sons, it is important to find an adult male—uncle, older brother, grandfather—who will be a stable male role model for the male child. If there is no adult male in the family who can fill this role, organizations such as the Big Brothers' program or the YMCA can help meet his needs. Or if a woman has a long-term relationship with a man who spends a considerable amount of time in her home, he could provide a masculine role model for her son.

Of equal significance is the way the opposite-sex parent interacts with a child in preparing him or her for dealing with the outside world. As a father, your attention to your daughter cues her on how to interact with men. If you say to your daughter, "That is a lovely dress. You certainly look beautiful tonight," she will begin to appreciate having a man flatter her. Her mother may say the same thing, but it will affect her differently. A kind word, a hug, and a kiss on the cheek from a father will let a young girl know that she can gain acceptance and appreciation from men.

Likewise, your son's relationship with his mother will determine how he interacts with females in his life. A boy who loves and respects his mother will develop positive feelings toward women and can become a very loving husband. However, if you, as a mother, are demanding in your relationship with your son, he may be obedient but resentful. He may then find it difficult to be attracted to any woman.

It is important for both parents to show a child of either sex that you care, to express and show your affection—but not to the point of being intimidating or annoying. Hugs and compliments work best when your child welcomes them, but too much affection may send some children—particularly in early adolescence—running from the room. Your child's reaction will tell you how much physical affection he wants.

Children can also learn about their gender roles by interacting with other children in the family. It is important for you to remember that a clear sense of sexual identity is crucial for passing through puberty with a minimum of emotional scarring. *If your child is displaying difficulty with fulfilling his sex-linked roles, either socially or in the family, he may be having a gender role problem.* Speak to your child about your concerns. (The guidelines on active listening from the companion volume *Creating a Good Self-Image in Your Child* would be helpful in this case.) If you are unable to solve the problem together, therapy might be necessary.

Too often it is only when children have difficulties in adolescence that their parents realize there had been a problem much further back in childhood. By then, however, it is too late—either to apply lethal doses of discipline or to suddenly reform as parents and become exemplary models of what you would like your children to be. Family ties must be developed from the day of birth. If you continuously serve as a good role model, show sincere interest in your children, and validate them as human beings, you will be building respect and love—and the caring necessary to bind the family together. The final part of this book explains how you can help precipitate this happy result.

Part III
Some Strategies for Maximizing Your Role Modeling

There are a number of basic areas you need to be aware of in the process of role modeling—from adopting the correct behavior to keeping the channels of communication open to understanding the most effective way to constructively criticize and nurture your child. The following suggestions will provide you with basic strategies; your own common sense will help you establish your own methods for implementing them.

STRATEGIES FOR CONSCIENTIOUS ROLE MODELING

HELPFUL HINT #1—DEMONSTRATE GOOD SPEECH AND ENCOURAGE FAMILY INTERACTION AND COMMUNICATION

Language is the single most important factor influencing academic success and future achievement. Children learn their language skills primarily from their parents. Although we usually think of language as being taught in school, most children bring to school the language they have already acquired at home. Depending on his age and capabilities, your child enters school with a certain degree of word mastery and a syntax for combining words and concepts. The more sophisticated his speech and vocabulary, and the greater his understanding of language, the more he will profit from school.

A child who has learned to listen because you involve him in conversation is better able to follow verbal directions in school. A child whose parents have read to him will have learned to attend more closely to speech. If communication in your family allows for the free flow of conversation and provides all family members, including your child, the opportunity to speak, be heard, and have others respond to what he says, he will develop the skill of good listening, which is essential to success in the classroom.

A child who hears only insults and criticism or is verbally harassed at home will "tune out." In a family such as Susan and Eileen's, for example, where the parents constantly nagged each other, the children actually learned to stop listening. If your family life involves this kind of perpetual argument or nagging, your child may simply avoid being drawn into the situation by actually learning *not* to listen. Such a child will find it difficult to focus on speech at school. He will be unable to follow verbal instructions and to understand classroom instruction.

Because your child learns to speak by having opportunities to talk to someone who will listen, he needs to find encouragement and respect for what he has to say. Many parents, overloaded with their own concerns, forget the importance of the simple act of listening to their children, as well as the feedback that says more than anything else to the child, "I heard you." You can help your child simply by listening to what he has to say and by encouraging him to verbalize his thoughts. Being tolerant, rather than critical, of your child's conversation is essential. No child is going to be able to communicate on an adult level, and you should not expect this. Nor, on the other hand, should you talk down to your child; using baby talk will hardly encourage mature speech. It requires some balance and fine-tuning, but it is important to your child's development. The language skills and communication modeling you do will be of vital importance to your child's future success.

There is no doubt that language is the basis for reading. A child whose language development is delayed cannot follow teachers' directions and does not understand what he reads. A child who lacks good verbal skills and has not learned to listen and use information will be at a severe disadvantage when it comes time to learn to read. Michael, for example, developed a severe learning problem because he was raised in a large, hectic home where family members had little time for interpersonal interaction. Michael's parents were immigrants from a small village in northern Italy. They worked hard to support their family, which was large and always growing. At the time Michael entered therapy, there were fifteen children living at home. A family pattern became established where the infants and younger children were left in the care of the older children.

Michael, who fell somewhere in the middle of the family, was a silent child. His teachers could not induce him to speak in class. In fact, they reported that he was never heard to speak at all. Some school personnel felt that Michael might be retarded or suffering from a learning disability. His situation was so bad that he was unable to follow simple directions and his work suffered greatly. In therapy Michael finally was able to describe how he felt. He said that nobody paid any attention to him. There were just too many children for his parents to handle, and his older siblings were too busy taking care of themselves or the new babies. He had no one to talk to and so, he thought, no reason to talk.

It was not that Michael couldn't talk but that he had so few experiences in expressing himself that his language skills were primitive. He did not lack body language and understanding of language basics; but his home life had led him to withdraw. While he was in therapy, Michael was also tested and proved to be of average intelligence. He was referred for special work in listening and expression and eventually performed schoolwork at grade level.

Although Michael's case is extreme, it illustrates how important it is for you to allow—and encourage—your child to express himself in the home. Only then will he have the confidence and skills to interact with others.

Communication is the very heart of family interaction. Many more problems could be solved within families if only family members would communicate with each other beyond the level of "Hey, cut it out!" or "Stop that. Pick up your clothes." Your child models his speech on what he hears at home. There are a number of simple approaches you can implement to provide the proper environment for language development.

Actively Engage Your Child in Conversation

Speak to your child—not merely to say "It's time for bed" or "Come to dinner." Draw your child into conversations on subjects that are of interest to him and encourage him to express his own opinions. Above all, respect what your child says and listen patiently to his ideas. A child requires time to organize his thoughts, so you must be prepared to be patient. Cutting a child off before he has finished speaking, or interrupting a train of thought by summarizing what he is trying to say, will discourage further attempts at communication and undermine language development. It may even cause the child to stutter. It is a sad fact of contemporary American life that many of our children may lack sufficient opportunity to speak at home and enter school with unnecessarily limited language capability, which causes them to be ashamed to volunteer in class or extracurricular activities. This in turn further retards their ability to learn.

Speak in Full Sentences and Express Complete Ideas

Often parents make the mistake of changing their

speech patterns when they talk to their children. They drop the more formal, enriched speech they use with each other and with other adults and talk in phrases rather than complete sentences. This is a grave error. If you do this, what you are teaching your child is communication that lacks good structure, has little enriching vocabulary, and, most of all, allows for incomplete expressions of ideas. If you want your child to have a strong vocabulary, you must use the words you want him to use. And never forget that your child is always listening—even as you speak to someone else in the family. When you and your spouse speak to each other, your child will listen for new words and sentence constructions, as well as to the overall tone of the conversation.

Be Specific in What You Say and What You Mean

Rather than saying, "Boy, that was really nice," speak clearly and specifically, with the vocabulary that will help your child in school (and that you would prefer that he use around the house). For example, take this imaginary dialogue between a mother and her four-year-old daughter.

Mother: *Cindi, the way you set the table looked* beautiful. *I appreciate your helping me.*
Cindi: *Thanks, Mom. But what does beautiful mean?*
Mother: *It means that the way you put things out makes the table pretty to look at.*

You should be as specific as possible when you

model words for your child, especially when you are praising—or reprimanding—your child's behavior. Avoid the use of vague words like *nice* and *OK* and substitute words that have real meaning and are more descriptive, such as *exciting, pleasant,* and *helpful.* Specific, clear expression is one of the most difficult things for anyone to learn. Learning begins with modeling in the home.

Never Deride Your Child's Speech or Rush Him in His Initial Efforts

The result of impatience with your child's speech in the early years is almost inevitably a child who stammers. As mentioned previously, a child needs time to organize his thoughts. If a young child just learning to speak begins with a lot of hesitation and verbal posturing—a "hum" or excessive "uhs" and "ums"—it is better to wait patiently, showing rapt attention. If you say such things as "Well, spit it out; what is it?" almost invariably the child will become an anxious speaker. The "uhs" and "ums" will not disappear but will instead become more hurried and jumbled.

It is often routine, especially if one or both parents are absent during the day, to ask a child, "How was your day?" This provides a wonderful opportunity for your child to practice his language skills because it allows him to pick and choose his subject matter and to express himself freely. He is not being asked to justify an action or to describe something that is important to you. When you do ask your child, however, be prepared to listen. One shy six-year-old was referred to therapy because of his difficulty in communicating with teachers and other adults. After some discussion, it surfaced that his father had a routine of coming home after work and at the dinner table perfunctorily asking the children, "How was your day?" Before the children could finish responding, however, he would open the newspaper and read, oblivious of all else. The children were left talking to the front page. What the children gathered from their father's behavior was that what they had to say was really not important. Although verbally their father was indicating interest, his behavior was communicating indifference. This is another example of double messages parents sometimes express. Always remember that your behavior counts more in influencing your child than what you say.

Avoid Baby Talk

Baby talk deserves special consideration. Many parents are unaware that when they use baby talk with their children they are actually encouraging backward behavior. *There are no circumstances under which it's desirable for an adult to use baby talk with a child.* It is one thing to be able to understand a young child's gestures and follow the child's initial attempts at speaking, but a parent who is interested in being a good role model will not mimic a young child's broken speech.

For example, if two-year-old Millie says, "Cookie—me," mother should say, "Baby wants a cookie" or even "Do you want a cookie?" Or when Millie says, "Me go too," mother should say, "You want to go to the store with me?"

In this way you set the example of always enriching your child's expression, without making him feel bad about his attempt to express himself. You have repeated the child's message in a full sentence, which shows him how to express his wants and ideas thoroughly. Rather than relying on other people to interpret what he says, he will be able to express himself clearly.

Thus, while it is normal for a child to begin talking what we refer to as baby talk, it is not advisable that you communicate with even your younger children in this manner. When you or other caretakers in the child's environment speak to him this way, you are actually modeling undesirable backsliding behavior. A young child needs to develop his physical speech faculties and may make noises and talk gibberish. But if you and other adults encourage this sort of behavior, your child will learn that this is cute and may not move on to more mature means of self-expression. Even when an infant gestures and makes noises, you can begin modeling proper expression and aiding language development by actually saying what the baby wants. When an infant cries, for example, ask, "You want Mama to take you out of the crib?" Thus, instead of attempting to stifle this primitive attempt at communication, you are saying in a comforting manner what the infant seems to be expressing. In this way, it is possible to begin teaching good verbal expression in infancy.

By the time your child is able to speak even a little (certainly by age twelve months he should be able to make hard consonant sounds, like *k*), you should no longer respond to gestures alone. If the child says, "Kuh," you might ask, "Do you mean *cup*?" clearly emphasizing the word you want the child to say. Or you might ask questions using the same emphasis: "Oh, you want to sit in your *chair?*" But you should no longer respond to such gestures as gesturing, tugging, pointing, and incoherent whining. Once your child has reached the point where he can label things, you can say, "I don't know what you mean. You'll have to say it for me." As much as possible, require the child to speak for himself.

If your child knows how to speak well but slips back into baby talk, you might respond by saying, "When you speak like that, I really can't understand you. Please tell me clearly what you mean." By all means avoid saying things like "You're being silly" or "You know better than that." Always remember to respect and honor your child's efforts and be aware that a certain amount of backsliding is inevitable. Communication is one of the most important skills you can give to your child, and you must strive to make the expression of emotions, experiences, and ideas a comfortable experience for all members of your family.

HELPFUL HINT #2—RESPECT AND ENCOURAGE YOUR CHILD'S INITIATIVE

Respecting what your child says involves not only listening to what he says in conversations you initiate but also listening to the topics he brings up.

Often parents believe it is their role to cultivate a young mind and lead him to sophisticated language by setting an example at the dinner table or elsewhere. If this is achieved by carefully contrived rules that actually limit discussion, it is done at the expense of a child's initiative.

Linda's family, for example, had very formal dinners with all five children present. It was supposed to be a time for family discussions, but Linda's father was a very dogmatic person and decreed that only certain topics were acceptable for dinnertime conversation. Mostly these were topics that the father could prove himself knowledgeable about or that *he* considered acceptable conversation for the dinner table. Because the family was large and both parents were very busy, this was the only time that the entire group was assembled. It would have provided an excellent time to practice family communication patterns. By being so rigid and controlling in this situation, Linda's father was actually modeling negative communication and downgrading some of the subjects that were obviously important to the children.

Rather than limit what can be discussed at the dinner table or try to force your child into what you consider elevated discussions, it is better to start with what the child is genuinely interested in. From a foundation of ordinary experience and personal interest, you can point out or direct the conversation to less obvious, more advanced levels of understanding. If your son comes home and says at dinner, "This kid kicked me in school," you can develop this piece of experience through natural conversation into a discussion of aggressiveness. But first acknowledge the worth of what the child is telling you. Express interest in the details; ask questions: "Were you hurt? You seem to be all right now. I wish you had told me earlier; that must have hurt. Did he kick you hard? How did it happen?"

Good teaching starts where the child is at any given moment and proceeds from there. If you would like your child to speak with mature, sophisticated words and sentences about far-reaching ideas, not only do you have to use the vocabulary and syntax you expect, but you must also involve the child in using such language. Interest is the surest way to gain involvement. Start with what the child knows, the topics he wishes to talk about. Your child will learn that ordinary things are worth discussing intelligently and that experience can be the basis for further thought. You may find that what interests him can be of interest to you.

Remember that you are not in competition with your child. You need not show that you know more than he does. An uncritical approach is needed. You should compliment your child when he has done well—and you should do so eagerly and share jubilantly in your child's successes. In speaking and listening skills, this means respecting what your child says, praising his efforts, and pointing out, however small it may seem, what he has done right. In this way, you can encourage your child to speak, and you will aid his later success in school and throughout life.

HELPFUL HINT #3—ALWAYS MODEL THE BEHAVIOR YOU WISH YOUR CHILD TO IMITATE

We have stated the fundamental principle of doing what you want your child to do rather than merely telling him what to do. There are probably few people who would argue with the logic of this statement. You should not feel discouraged, however, if you approach this with a fair amount of trepidation. If you are taking on the responsibility of rearing a child, it is a formidable but necessary task to act in the way you wish him to function.

Perhaps the first thing you must understand is that modeling the correct behavior for your child may require you to make some changes in how you live your own life. There is no other factor that is more important for your child than the behavior you demonstrate in the home. You have a tremendously influential role in your child's development at all ages. You cannot mindlessly engage in behavior without assessing how it will affect your child. This means having an awareness of what you do and what kind of example you are setting. This will change as your child grows because there will be different kinds of behavior he will be more tuned into depending on his own interests and the interests of his peers. Something that may have escaped him at five may become all-important at ten. The fact that Daddy plays baseball may be of no significance to a three-year-old but may become an important part of role modeling when at twelve he tries to decide whether to go out for track or the baseball team.

Industry and Perseverance

Most parents would like to see their children work hard and succeed in school and later in a career. The model that you present is the most effective means of ensuring this success. A child whose parents work hard sees by their example that hard work is the preferred lifestyle. The child understands from the very earliest that to get anywhere or achieve anything he has to make a commitment of time, effort, and emotion.

In families and cultures where industriousness is the unspoken rule and parents work hard at what they do, children learn that personal effort does count for something. When parents work and succeed because of their efforts, children imitate that lifestyle.

Working hard in your career and succeeding will not ensure that your child will work hard and succeed in school and in his career. Bonding within the family must be strong for a child to identify with you and your values. If your relationship is strong and your child feels he is a valued member of the family, he will follow your role modeling. When bonding is weak—particularly if your career interferes with time spent with the child—he will not identify with your example. Your child will not pick up your values unless you spend time together.

If your family has a habit of constantly blaming

outside forces—luck or fate—instead of taking responsibility for your own successes and failures, you are modeling the wrong behavior. If your child fails in school, and you say it is the teacher's fault, not the child's responsibility. If Mom or Dad is late for an appointment, you blame it on the car or traffic or the weather. This sets a bad example for a child. He learns to think of himself as a victim of all kinds of external forces. Instead of taking control of his life, he gets in the habit of attributing everything that happens, good or bad, to events and people beyond his control. You should take responsibility for your life so that your child learns to take responsibility for his.

Frugality and Fiscal Responsibility

How can an affluent parent serve as an effective role model for his child—so that the child will work hard in school and in a career? Though they usually have more than their basic needs provided for them, children of wealthier families need not grow up as lazy, irresponsible, and wasteful, as so many books, TV shows, and movies would have us believe. Your child learns moderation from you. If bonding is strong and you live moderately, your child will avoid overindulgence. Eating, drinking, and spending in moderation will communicate to your child that a moderate lifestyle—not the jet-set fantasy of TV shows and movies—is normal.

If you are always shopping, buying sports cars and expensive clothing—whenever and whatever you want just because you want it—your child will learn to expect the same. Of course, you need not wear rags and live in a hovel, but as with all role modeling, be aware of what you do and of what message this sends to your child.

A child who no sooner voices a desire than it is fulfilled feels his every whim should immediately be gratified. He has no experience in putting off desires until later. He may be successful in school, but he learns to be impulsive and indulgent in his desires. In a career one cannot expect immediate gratification. As adults we know we must often defer goals for the sake of immediate necessities. Sometimes it's a long time before success, material or other, is attained. A child who has been indulged is not used to waiting and may not understand or know how to cope with these conditions. Providing too much for your child certainly can sap his ambition.

Aggression

Children are aggressive in interactions with others as an extension of the aggression they see at home. If parents constantly yell at each other, their children, or others outside the family, their child will do the same thing. If, in response to this, parents punish a child, he will stop that aggression at home but become more abusive with friends outside the home.

Children and parents do, of course, become frustrated and even angry with one another. You have to sit down with the child and find out why he is so angry. Name-calling is a sign of hostility. If clear lines of communication exist in a family, those times when members do get angry can be handled effectively through discussion when all parties are calm and rational. You and your child need to establish a relationship in which you can discuss emotions together. If your child has said something mean to you, you might say, "Your language shows a lot of anger toward me. I feel bad about this; let's sit down and talk. Is there something I did wrong?" After the problem has been discussed fully in an honest, caring manner, you could say, "I'm sorry I made you feel so angry," and hopefully the child will apologize as well. At these times, positive physical contact is important—a hug or a kiss to show you do care and value your child as a person. You might affirm your feelings verbally, too: "You know I love you and would not do anything to hurt you intentionally. I'm sorry." In this way, a potentially volatile situation can be turned into further strengthening of family ties. If a child is consistently hostile toward his parents, professional intervention may be needed.

If parents use physical abuse in interacting with each other, their children, or other people, it will promote physical aggression in the children. If you are aggressive in everyday situations—dealing with store clerks and bank tellers, driving on the road—your child is likely to grow up believing that aggression is an acceptable way of interacting. Your child will absorb these behavior patterns and will employ them when interacting with peers.

Some parents will try to exert a more direct influence. A father may advise his son to go after a child who has hurt him. "Don't let him get away with it!" he will say or "Clobber that jerk." Such advice promotes violent aggression in the child. If such a father thinks that aggression will be limited to that situation, he should think again. A child so encouraged will be aggressive everywhere, in public and personal interactions, including within the family.

Once a pattern of aggressive behavior is set in motion, you will not be able to limit it with punishment or by verbal commands. Physical punishment will only fuel the pattern of aggression. A cycle will develop in which the parent continues to model aggression and the child continues to behave aggressively, further requiring the parent to be that much more aggressive in controlling him. The result is an unending pattern of hostility and aggression.

Substance Abuse

There are specific behaviors that have serious repercussions on a social level when modeled to your child. We are speaking especially of substance abuse. Drug addiction is a serious problem that affects children at all socioeconomic levels. The one most consistent cause of drug addiction or substance abuse of any kind by children is the model parents provide. Drinking is certainly one way parents influence their children. Parents who smoke can expect their children to try cigarettes by as young as age six, when parental behaviors have become internalized. The same is true of most other addictive habits.

This may ask a great deal of you—to become aware of your habits and, in some cases, change your lifestyle. However, this is what being an effective role model entails. Although many parents blame a child's bad habits on his friends, it is behavior that is modeled and sanctioned in the home that may actually lead a child to become involved in negative behavior outside of the family. This does not mean that in every family where the parents drink alcohol there will be a substance abuse problem. Engaging in any kind of behavior, be it a cocktail before dinner or a cigarette after, however, does suggest to the child that the behavior is OK.

Frank, a young high school senior, was referred to therapy because his teachers had noticed that he was often absent from school and often appeared to be in ill health. In therapy Frank admitted that he was drinking up to three six-packs of beer even on school nights. He had watched his father sit in front of the television night after night and drink a six-pack of beer by himself. He had always admired his father for consuming a six-pack at one sitting and set out to imitate the behavior as proof of his own self-worth. The problem was complicated by the fact that his father often bragged about his consumption to his son—even though Frank's mother tried to encourage her son to wait until he was older before he started drinking. Frank was unaware that each beer he drank contained one ounce of alcohol, which meant that a six-pack was equivalent to almost half a pint of vodka or whiskey. Frank—and his father—were also unaware that alcohol kills the male hormone testosterone.

Frank's father's message to his son was that beer drinking is basically harmless and something to be proud of. In therapy Frank was encouraged to identify aspects about himself that he felt good about and other aspects of his father's behavior that he could model and excel at in order to win his father's affection and admiration.

It is interesting to note that such potentially negative behavior often falls along sexual lines. Daughters will follow their mother's lead, sons their father's. It is still less likely today for women to drink as much as men. Although this is changing somewhat, there remains in our culture a masculine mystique about being able to consume large quantities of alcohol. Young adolescent girls may not refuse a single beer at a party, but it is less likely that they will drink—as is not uncommon for boys of the same age—an entire six-pack in an evening.

Depending on your community and the values of your child's peer groups, as well as the availability of alcohol in the home, a child may experiment with drinking as early as age six or eight, especially if he is encouraged to do so by his peers. It is important to note, however, that if you have been attentive to your child, have modeled good and reasonable behavior, and have acted as a concerned and caring individual, you will be one step ahead of the game when your child is faced with such temptations. (Parents may want to consult a companion book in this series, *Helping Your Child Cope with Peer Pressure*, for a further discussion of this subject.)

It is also important to note that not every child who experiments with drugs or alcohol will become a substance abuser or even a regular user. In fact, as we indicated in the previous section, substance abuse—drugs, alcohol, or even cigarettes—can be a sign that your child is having role problems, and you are advised to seek professional help.

We are not advocating that you give up drinking, but we are suggesting that you become aware of yourself and your habits, especially when your child is present. You may attempt to make verbal directions contrary to your actions; "Don't drink beer; it's not good for you." But your child will do what you do, rather than as you say. Keep liquor locked up, as young children are naturally curious and will experiment with whatever is available to them. Even if you keep liquor on hand only for company, you should be sure to take precautions. There is a difference between total abstinence and setting an example of moderation. If a father drinks beer in his child's presence, he might want to limit himself to one or two beers in the course of a meal or a television program. If a mother is in the habit of taking a martini or a glass of wine when she gets home from work each day, she should be sure that it doesn't interfere with the family. Families who drink wine with meals might take the time to explain to their children why wine is a beverage to be enjoyed with food.

Parents who use tranquilizers and other drugs are wise to keep drugs out of the reach of children. A child's natural curiosity knows no danger; he will want to try what he sees you doing. If you are on medication, avoid broadcasting this to your child. Don't exclaim in front of your child, "Oh, I need my tranquilizers! How could I get through the day without them?" Or in talking to your spouse in front of your child, don't discuss the prescribed medication you may be taking, complaining, "I took my sleeping pill last night and it didn't work; I'll have to take two tonight." This goes for all medication, including prescription drugs, such as antibiotics, and over-the-counter medicine, such as aspirin. Our culture is drug-dependent on many levels, and a child need not necessarily observe you using an illegal drug to think that drug use is fine. An atmosphere of pill popping in the home may induce the child to experiment. Thus if for some reason you find it necessary to take medication, make it a private affair and keep all medicine out of the reach of your child.

HELPFUL HINT #4—ALWAYS BE CLEAR IN EXPRESSING YOUR EMOTIONAL REACTIONS TO YOUR CHILD

To effectively role-model handling and expressing emotions, you should express how you feel as honestly and as clearly as possible. You should be careful, however, always to differentiate your dissatisfaction with your child's behavior from the child as a person. If your child does something disagreeable or contrary to the rules and values of the family, you should discuss the *behavior*, not the *child*. To say to a child, "You are a bad boy" is a sweeping statement that attacks the child's developing sense of self-worth. Be specific about what the child did that was "bad," whether it be forgetting to put his crayons away or hitting his sister over the head with the crayon box. Any disciplinary action should never be expressed as "I'm sick of you" or "You make me so angry; get out of my sight." Blaming or personally attacking the child when you express your emotions only serves to erode your child's self-esteem. And a child with a weak sense of self-worth will be prey for every bad influence that comes along, because he will not have the strength to resist; he will not have the firm foundation of a secure home life to rely on for strength and values.

In general, it is always best to avoid placing blame too emphatically, especially when you do not know for certain where it lies. Often parents will force a child to claim responsibility for bad or unacceptable behavior, even if they are not sure whose fault it is. This sets a bad example for the child, who will think placing blame is more important than doing the right thing. More often than not, when parents try to place blame without actually knowing who was responsible by the offending act, they accuse the wrong child or make false accusations. *A wrongly accused child will have doubts about fair treatment inside the family as well as in the world.* Such a child becomes resentful of all parental actions, will challenge parents' authority even when parents are right, and will rebel against family values. He may purposely seek out situations that are wrong. In reality there is no need to place blame. Blaming is not positive in any way. It is far better to sit down with those involved and discuss what went on, respecting what the child or children have to say. Pointing a finger or establishing guilt is irrelevant.

You should also learn to express your feelings and the need for discipline in carefully worded statements, such as, "When you did . . . , it made me feel. . . ." This is also the case when expressing positive feelings. Specify that you think Jamie was a good boy because he remembered to brush his teeth right after lunch. Your child will learn from your example to identify and speak about his feelings rather than to keep emotions inside and act out in other ways. The inability to express emotion is a prime factor in depression among teenagers. (And depression is one of the factors in a rising rate of teenage suicides.) If a child is not allowed or unable to express strong feelings at any age, he will hold them inside and brood. Eventually the effort to keep the feelings bottled up becomes too much; the child may decide that he cannot take any more and wants out. Again, as we said in Part Two, a child who is continually withdrawn or depressed is sending you a message. Pay attention and take steps to help him.

You should feel comfortable expressing strong emotions openly and honestly to your family. Your behavior and means of expression will set the proper example for your child. Saying "I love you" should not be difficult. Sincere, positive remarks such as "I am glad to see you" or "Looking at you and being with you is wonderful" are laudable as a daily occurrence in a family. A mother who takes the time to tell her six-year-old, "I'm very happy you're home from school. Come give me a hug" or "I'm glad to be home from work so I can spend time with you" will not only be expressing her feelings; she will be communicating her love to her child. The child will respond to both the intention and the message of her thoughtful act.

Communication of emotions is crucial, especially if the emotions are those we usually refer to as negative—anger, fear, or frustration. Your child has to learn how to express such feelings to others in a positive manner, and you must take the initiative to set the example for effective expression. Negative emotions should be expressed carefully, openly, clearly, using such specific language as "When you did . . . , you really hurt my feelings," "I worry about you when you stay out late and don't call," or "I am angry with this sort of behavior." (With this last, it is better to be as exact as possible.) Even negative emotions can be expressed without blaming, in such a way that your child knows you love him and dislike only *what he is doing.* Most children want only approval and love. They do not delight in doing destructive things. Only a child who has been hurt delights in destructive actions. Again, such a child is troubled and needs special care.

HELPFUL HINT #5—MAKE A POINT OF ADMITTING YOUR ERRORS

Parents make mistakes. A child, of course, knows this but may be afraid to take issue with his parents. If you are willing to admit your errors and take full responsibility for them, your child will learn to take responsibility and admit his own mistakes. On the other hand, your child will learn to deny stubbornly that he has done something wrong, blame his problems on outside factors, and place responsibility outside his control if those are the behaviors he sees you practicing.

This is a common flashpoint for disputes within families. A parent may say, "I saw you spill the milk." The child might respond, "No, I didn't do it," even though it's obvious the child did spill the milk. These kinds of arguments are common to families in which the parents have made mistakes, often as trivial as spilling in the kitchen, and refuse—sometimes vehemently—to admit error. Spills are a minor matter, but if parents cannot admit their fallibility in trivial areas, they will even more strongly resist admitting their responsibility in more significant situations.

Some parents want to save face in the presence of their children and are unable to own up to being imperfect, for fear of undermining their power as positive role models. But being able to say to your child, "I was wrong" sets a more self-assured and beneficial example—for life both in the family and in society—than unyieldingly insisting you could not have made a mistake. You do not have to prove your authority; the child knows that without you he cannot survive.

Often parents complain that their children fail to hold themselves accountable for mistakes or decisions. This failure to take responsibility and control is often the result of poor role modeling. What happens is that problems are swept under the rug, so to speak, and the child learns that it is better not to admit when he has done something wrong—it is better not to hold himself accountable for failure—but to deny it or to blame it on outside circumstances. *When mistakes are always attributed to outside forces, your child can't learn from his errors, so he repeats them again and again.* Unfortunately, this eventually leads to a feeling of powerlessness in a world where outside events dictate failure and success. The ultimate result for a child who learns this kind of behavior is that he will shirk responsibility and will most likely fail to make a success of himself.

It takes a great deal of self-esteem and self-assurance to admit you were wrong, to accept responsibility. But it is extremely important that you do so. When accidents occur or you find yourself in the wrong, what can you do as an effective role model? Admit your error and apologize. "The accident was my fault," you might say, or "I was wrong for blaming you. Will you forgive me?" Asking your child's forgiveness, when the situation calls for it, will teach the child to do the same—to admit mistakes and ask for forgiveness. Your child will imitate what he sees you do; this point cannot be emphasized enough. *The power of saying "I'm sorry" should never be underrated. Rather than undermining your authority, being able to admit mistakes actually brings you closer to your children.* As an expression of love, saying you are sorry can be the cement that bonds the family together. The result will be trust and forgiveness from your child. A parent who consistently denies guilt triggers defensive reactions in a child— sometimes even when the parent is innocent. When you have made a real mistake, view it as an opportunity for bonding with your child, for learning and teaching acceptance of responsibility.

Very young children, from eighteen months to age four or five, do not have the ego strength to admit having made a mistake. A child this young is in the initial stages of developing a value system; he has not yet internalized standards for success and failure. Thus he will not have a strong enough sense of self to take active responsibility for himself.

Denial of mistakes will be natural. He will cover up his errors or lie, and he should not be severely reprimanded for doing so. Although the importance of telling the truth should always be emphasized, you should strive to draw an explanation from your child rather than accuse him of lying. Denial is one of the earliest defenses developed in human beings and remains with us even as adults. Do not be overly critical of it in your child. (A more detailed discussion of the behavioral standards appropriate to the stages of childhood development is available in the companion volume *Creating a Good Self-Image in Your Child.*)

Unfortunately, older children and adults also use denial. Denial is not appropriate behavior for adults. When you deny what is real, you actively distort reality. Adolescents and adults who rely on denial need help. If a child younger than age five uses it, he can be excused. Although you should not attempt to force a child so young into accountability, you should remember that a young child is watching you even at that age, so the need for effective role modeling remains.

If a young child spills milk, throws something, hits

or pinches another child, rather than asking, "Did you do it?" you should use honest expression of emotions, saying, "When you throw your toys around, you know I have to clean them up, and I'm not happy about that." If you ask whether the child did it, he will most likely deny it. So rather than engage in an argument about your child's behavior, express what your feelings are in response to his actions. Avoid asking for acceptance of responsibility from a young child; he is not old enough. Instead of asking, "Did you pinch your sister?" to which the child is likely to respond, "No," even if you *saw* it, just say, "When you pinch your sister hard like that, you know she feels bad."

Lying or lying by omission is a constant in our society—the little white lie. A lie—no matter how small—is still a lie, however, and can severely affect open communication in the family. If you lie to family members or other people—especially in situations where your child knows you are lying—your child will do the same. Disciplinary measures such as admonishing or spanking the child will have little effect, except to weaken the bond between you and your child. If telling the truth is a clear ground rule and your child lies consistently, professional intervention may be needed. Strong discipline will do no good. The underlying reason for the child's lying must be discovered. There can be a host of causes you may not be aware of. Lying may be caused by many factors, from fear to anger. As we said previously, children with severe patterns of negative behavior may need professional help. This is true of stealing and other basically antisocial behaviors as

well. *These acts are symptoms of some other problem and are not the problem itself.* Stealing, for example, may be a symptom of a need for love. If the
behavior was picked up at home, it is imperative to
find out where it has come from and to remedy the
situation.

HELPFUL HINT #6—ALWAYS PROVIDE POSITIVE ENCOURAGEMENT

If you constantly criticize your child using such
phrases as, "You're lazy; you never do anything
right," your child will feel like an outcast at home.
All of us, adults and children alike, need a source of
positive input. If your child is constantly exposed to
negative criticism in the home, he will turn elsewhere—usually to peers—for the positive feedback
he needs. And it is in this type of a situation that a
child is likely to be heavily influenced by peer
groups and bow to demands that will assure his
group acceptance. If the bonding with peers requires the child to experiment with drugs, for example, he will be likely to do so in order to get the
acceptance and caring that are not provided at
home.

Your child's self-concept comes from feedback re-
ceived from you and other parental figures. Whenever you have a chance to praise your child, take
advantage of that opportunity. The more you do so,

the more closely your child will identify with you, with what you say, and with what you believe. Positive reinforcement goes a long way toward ensuring good behavior. *Your child will tend to duplicate behavior for which he is praised—more often than he will give up behavior he has been punished for or adopt good habits without praise. Focus on what your child does right and praise him often.*

As a parent you may often feel a spontaneous surge of love when your child is around—unconditionally, with no strings attached. We suggest that you give voice to this spontaneous affection as well as when the child has done something you approve of. Go to your child and say, "Let me just give you a hug right now"—for no apparent reason—or "It's so good to see you. I love you very much." You will find your child will be able to express strong, spontaneous, positive emotions effectively if you practice this.

You should also use positive physical contact as often as you praise your children verbally or express strong, positive emotions. Research has shown that infants need physical contact almost as much as they need food for healthy physical, psychological, and mental development. This need to be hugged and held remains important throughout a child's life. Don't be afraid to be affectionate with your spouse in front of your child. Hugging your spouse sets a good example for your child. Establishing positive physical contact as a regular form of expression in your home is not only good role modeling; it also builds self-esteem and reinforces your verbal messages to your child. *The combination of a firm, loving hug and words of love or praise spoken in strongly affectionate tones is incalculable—a potent medicine for dealing with immediate problems and a preventive measure to strengthen the family for future interaction.*

HELPFUL HINT #7—ACKNOWLEDGE YOUR CHILD'S FEARS

Children's fears are real to them. Do not discount them. A reasonable approach to such anxiety-producing situations as monsters in the dark or thunder and lightning sets a good example and helps diminish the power of these fears. Explaining the realities of the situation will help your child overcome those fears. You should never laugh at a child's fears or imply that he is silly or crazy to be afraid. Avoid belittling the fear as a means of alleviating it, even though your child's fears may seem absurd to you. To deal with such situations effectively you must first accept the reality of your child's fear, then help him understand not to be afraid. Poking fun at or making a joke of the fear will simply intensify it.

If, for example, your daughter thinks there is a bogeyman in the closet or a giant spider under the bed, the reasonable approach would be to turn on the lights and investigate with her. Expose the reality of the fear without belittling the child or discounting the potency of the fear. *Never, even in jest, suggest that the child is crazy. Your child's self-im-*

age reflects how he feels you perceive him. A child who is told he is crazy or unbalanced may begin to believe it.

If you model fear to your child, he will generally learn to feel fear in the same situations. If you are afraid of bugs or heights, your child will pick up on this. Children with severe phobias almost always have parents with severe phobias. In the case of a less severe fear, as with bugs, you should be aware that you can engender more severe fears in your child through your own inappropriate behavior. If you make a big deal of a spider, your child may believe he should have a strong fear of spiders. Such fears are not cute, and there is no reason to overreact unnecessarily to insignificant things.

HELPFUL HINT #8—MODEL SOLID PROBLEM-SOLVING SKILLS

An approach to problem solving that involves all family members is an excellent method for teaching problem-solving skills. In the family approach, your child participates in making decisions that concern the home life and the family. Since this method includes input from the child, it enhances his sense of self-worth and importance in the family. It also requires him to learn and practice a rational approach to problem solving, rather than merely accepting arbitrary decisions made by you or outside authorities.

This approach gives your child an opportunity to see you making decisions and to help you reach solutions. The example you set by using rational methods to discuss and examine issues will be useful to your child for the rest of his life.

HELPFUL HINT #9—FEEL COMFORTABLE SEEKING PROFESSIONAL HELP

Therapists often advise professional help to resolve family problems that can't be solved through conventional family dynamics. Briefly stated, there are two options for therapy: you may place the child in the individual care of a therapist, or the entire family may undergo therapy. The decision is based on the family at the time the decision for therapy is made. In some cases it might be detrimental for a troubled child to undergo sessions of family therapy because he might feel intimidated by the presence of his parents. In such instances, individual therapy may be more successful. Individual therapy—what is called *play therapy* for young children—allows a professional to observe your child and how problems manifest themselves in his behavior. Family therapy is preferable in other situations, especially as the child gets older. Older children have a sense of independence from parents and are able to stand up for their beliefs and actions, especially in the safety of a therapy session. If, for example, a parent attempts to stifle a child during the course of a therapeutic session, the therapist can intervene. This demonstrates to the child that the situation is not hopeless—that there are other adults in the world who are as powerful as his parent and who can intervene on his behalf.

Seeking therapy—whether as an individual or as a family—should be considered a normal part of maintaining family health and well-being. Unfortunately, therapy has been viewed too often as a sign of weakness when, in fact, *it takes courage to seek therapy—just as it requires intelligence and insight for you to realize that things may not be going well in the family.* Some parents fear involvement in therapy because it may uncover their own emotional problems; others falsely believe that therapy is only for "crazy" people. Today in our society people are beginning to understand that family therapy is actually just another service, in which professionals give advice to people who are interested in personal success in their lives. We readily accept advice from professionals in financial matters; we seek out doctors for our health. We take our cars to good mechanics for major jobs—though the responsibility for good driving remains in our hands after we leave the shop. Therapy and family counseling provide similar benefits.

CONCLUSION

In a sense, what we have been saying throughout this book is that you are what you do, and what you do will to a great extent determine what your child becomes. Undoubtedly, you want your child to become a confident, caring, successful person who espouses the values that are important to you. The best way to ensure that is to set a good example— not just when the moment seems right, but on a day-to-day basis from the moment your child is born.

In fact, you should envision yourself as a role model even before your child is born. Closely examine your values and attitudes and then take a long, hard look at yourself. Do you practice what you preach? If not, you'll be delivering conflicting messages to your child. It is only by sending consistent messages—through actions and words—to your child that you can share with him your values and attitudes and thus establish the parent-child bonding that will help your child develop self-confidence and a sense of self-worth.

Today's society makes more demands of parents—and thcir children—than ever before. Always being the type of person you wish your child to become can seem a formidable task at times, as can staying actively involved with your child. But quality time spent with your child is time well spent. Indeed, positive role modeling is the best preventive medicine available to you.

Actively encourage your child's initiative if you want him to succeed in life; be supportive and accepting, acknowledging his fears, applauding his achievements, and admitting your own errors. In doing so, you give him the love and respect he needs to become the best person he can be.

REFERENCES

Beckwith, Leila. "Caregiver-Infant Interaction and the Development of the High Risk Infant." *Intervention Strategies for High Risk Infants and Young Children.* Edited by Theodore Tjossem. Baltimore: University Park Press, 1976.

Berry, Mildred. *Language Disorders of Children.* New York: Meredith Corp., 1969.

Butterfield, E., and G. Cairns. "The Infant's Auditory Environment." *Intervention Strategies for High Risk Infants and Young Children.* Edited by Theodore Tjossem. Baltimore: University Park Press, 1976.

deQuiros, Julio. "Diagnosis of Vestibular Disorders in the Learning Disabled." *Journal of Learning Disabilities.* January 1976, vol. 9, no. 1.

Dougherty, Philip. "How Children Learn." *New York Times.* December 13, 1976.

Gesell, Arthur, and Frances Ild. *Infant and Child in the Culture of Today.* New York: Harper and Brothers, 1943.

Kappelman, Murray. "Prenatal and Perinatal Factors Which Influence Learning." *Exceptional Infant,* vol. 2. Edited by Jerome Hellmuth. New York: Brunner/Mazel, 1971.

Northern, Jerry, and M. Downs. *Hearing in Children.* Baltimore: Williams and Wilkins Co., 1974.

Parmelee, A., M. Sigman, C. Kopp, and A. Haber. "Diagnosis of the Infant at High Risk for Mental, Motor, and Sensory Handicaps." *Intervention Strategies for High Risk Infants and Young Children.* Edited by Theodore Tjossem. Baltimore: University Park Press, 1976.

Randolph, Theron. *Human Ecology and Susceptibility to the Environment.* Springfield, Ill.: Charles C. Thomas, 1962.

Rosner, Jerome. *Helping Children Overcome Learning Disabilities.* New York: Walker and Co., 1975.

Schecter, M., P. Toussieng, R. Sternlof, and E. Pollack. "Etiology of Mental Disorders: Prenatal, Natal and Postnatal Organic Factors." *Manual of Child Psychopathology.* New York: McGraw-Hill Book Co., 1972.

Stevens, Godfrey. "Early Intervention with High Risk Infants and Young Children: Implications for Education." *Intervention Strategies for High Risk*

Infants and Young Children. Edited by Theodore Tjossem. Baltimore: University Park Press, 1976.

Wunderlich, Ray. *Kids, Brains and Learning.* St. Petersburg, Fla.: Johnny Reads, 1970.